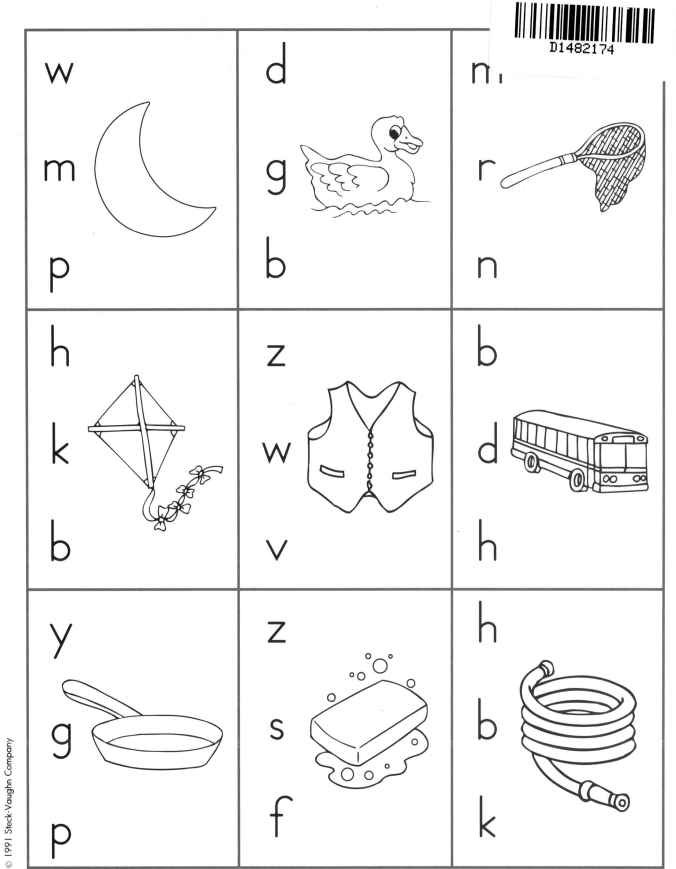

w	d	m
m	g	r
p	b	n

h	z	b
k	w	d
b	v	h

y	z	h
g	s	b
p	f	k

Name _____

Initial Consonants   Circle the letter that stands for the first sound in each picture name.

1

b d p g l t n v m

Final Consonants   Write the letter that stands for the last sound in each picture name.

b		l	
h		g	
f		k	

h		x	
t		s	
b		v	

d		k	
l		p	
t		g	

j		p	
y		v	
qu		g	

l		m	
f		r	
t		n	

f		m	
g		v	
z		r	

Name _____

Initial and Final Consonants Circle the letters that stand for the first sound and the last sound in each picture name.

e   **a**

e   i

u   **o**

a   i

u   **e**

u   **i**

u   **o**

a   e

e   i

4

Short Vowels Circle the letter that stands for the short vowel sound in each picture name.

© 1991 Steck-Vaughn Company

e i u	u e a	u a i
_____	_____	_____
_____	_____	_____
a o u	o a i	i e u
_____	_____	_____
_____	_____	_____
a o e	e u a	i u a
_____	_____	_____
_____	_____	_____

Name _____

Short Vowels Circle and write the letter that stands for the short vowel sound in each picture name.

5

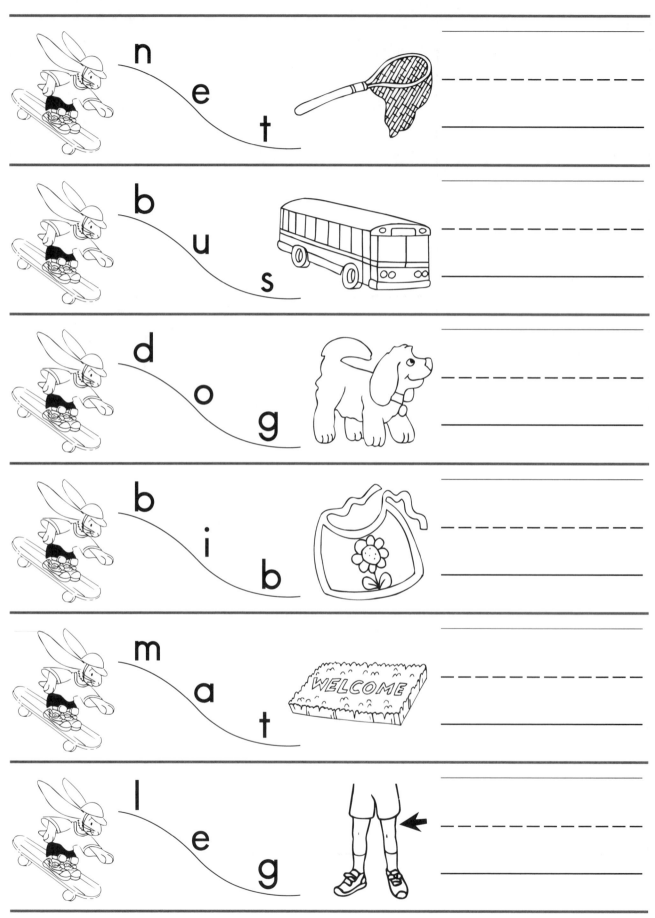

n e t

b u s

d o g

b i b

m a t

l e g

Blending Short Vowel Words Blend each word, and write it on the line.

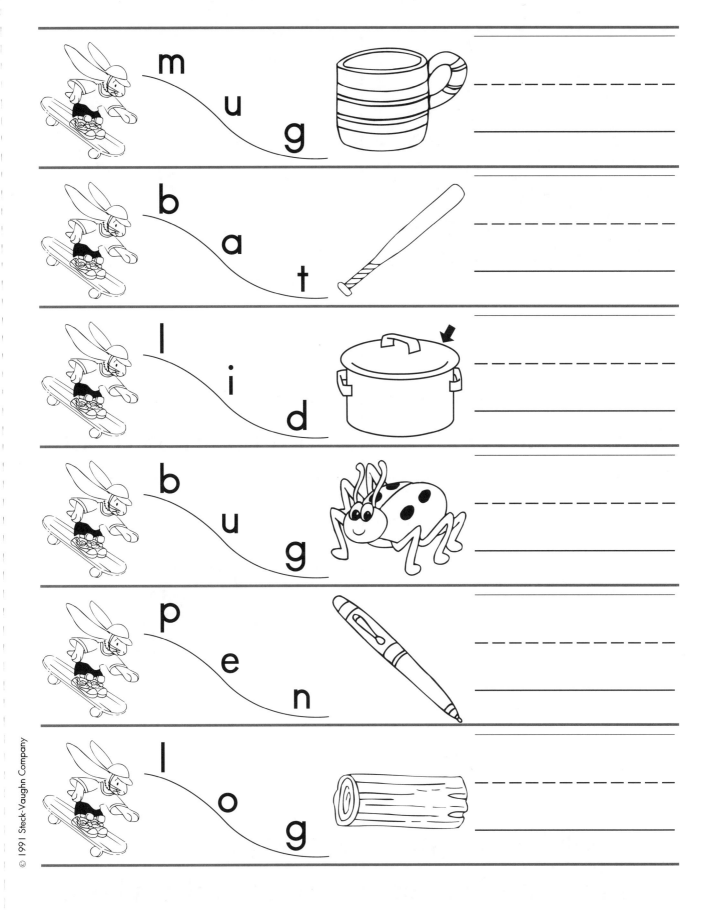

m u g

b a t

l i d

b u g

p e n

l o g

Name

Blending Short Vowel Words   Blend each word, and write it on the line.

Meg is not in the den.
Bob fed the dog.

A cat naps in the sun.
Dad set a lid on a pan.

Don will fix the rip.
The fox will dig a pit.

Ben has a wet cap.
Ten men had red hats.

Short Vowel Sentences   Underline the sentence that tells about each picture.

a　rake

Long a (cvce) Color the pictures whose names have the long *a* sound.

w a v e

c ___ p

l ___ k

g ___ t

v ___ s

c ___ n

Completing Long a Words (cvce)   Write *a_e* to complete each word whose name has the long *a* sound.

a

pail

Name _____

11

Long a (ai)   Color the pictures whose names have the long *a* sound.

r[ai]n

s____l

p____n

p____l

m____l

n____l

Completing Long a Words (ai) Write *ai* to complete each word whose name has the long *a* sound.

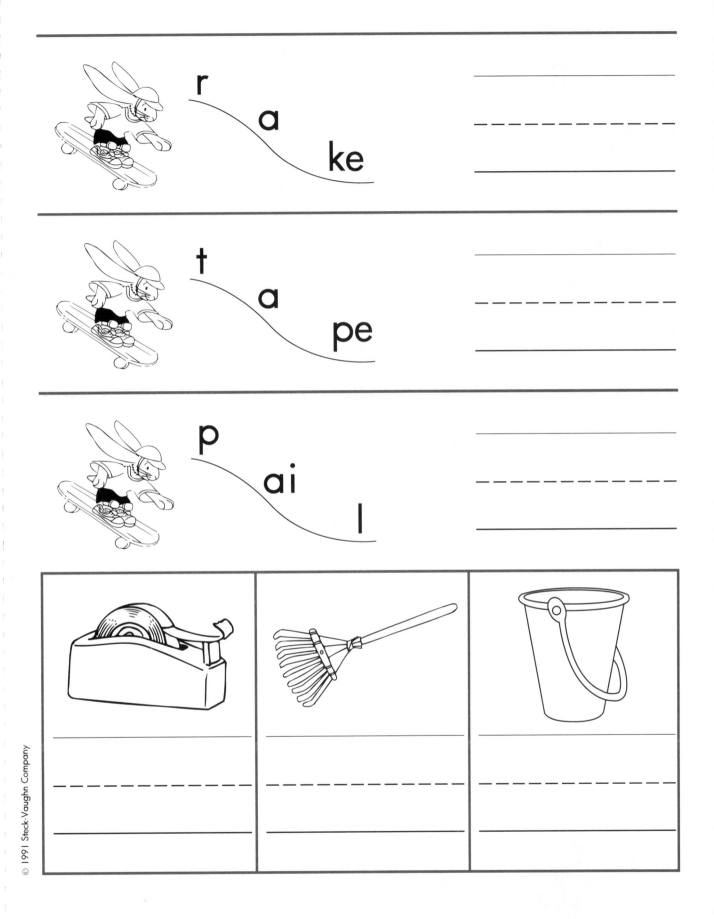

r a ke

t a pe

p ai l

Name _____

13

Blending Long a Words Blend each word, and write it on the line. Then write the word that names each picture.

p

ai

l

_____

- - - - - - - - -

tape
tag

nail
nap

tab
tail

lake
lap

rat
rake

sat
sail

sat
safe

cake
cat

Recognizing Long a Words Blend and write the first word. Then circle the word that names each picture.

Jane bakes a _____.

can   cake

Jane takes it to the _____.

lake   lap

The cake is in the _____.

ran   rain

Jane saves it with a _____.

pail   pad

Name _____

Completing Long a Sentences Write the word on the line that completes each sentence.

Kate has a pail of bait.
Dave had a cake sale.

Gail came with a game.
Jake wades in the lake.

Dale can bake a cake.
Dave has a tan cape.

Jake waits for the mail.
Jane waits in the rain.

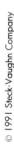

Long a Sentences   Underline the sentence that tells about each picture.

i   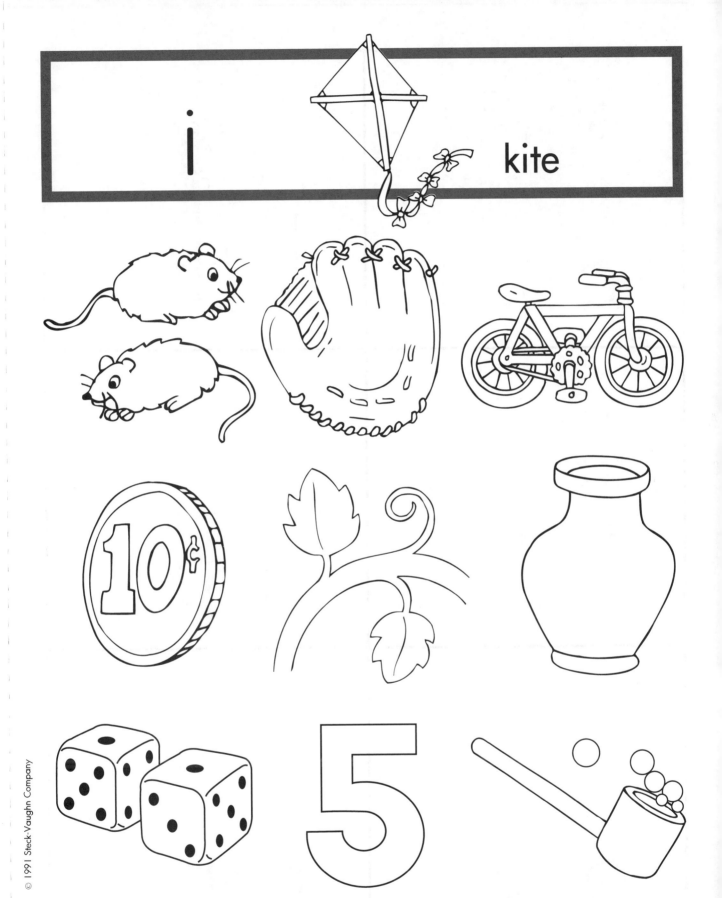   kite

Name _____

17

Long i (cvce)   Color the pictures whose names have the long *i* sound.

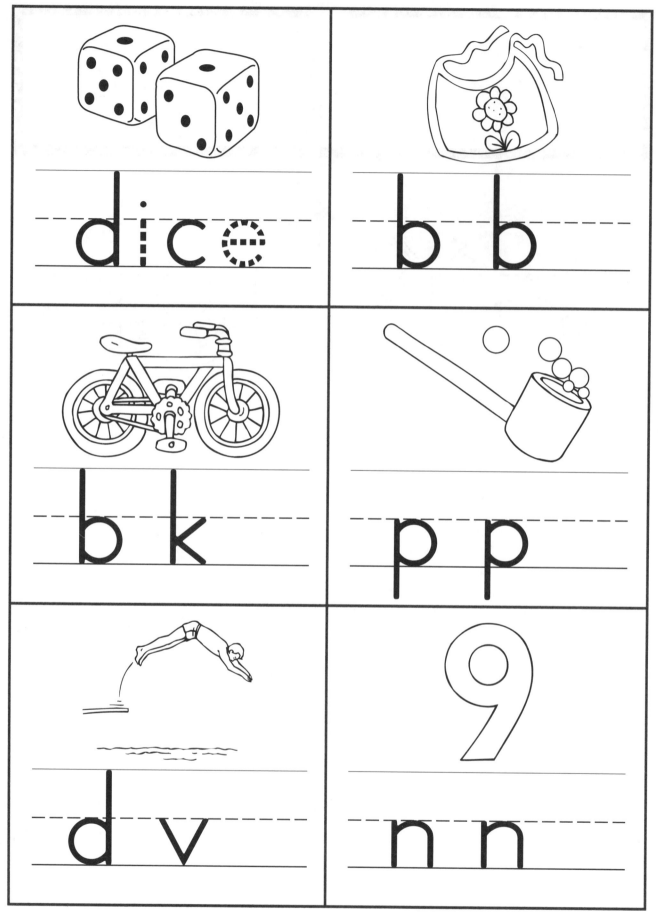

d i c e

b ___ b

b ___ k

p ___ p

d ___ v

n ___ n

18   **Completing Long i Words (cvce)**   Write *i_e* to complete each word whose name has the long *i* sound.

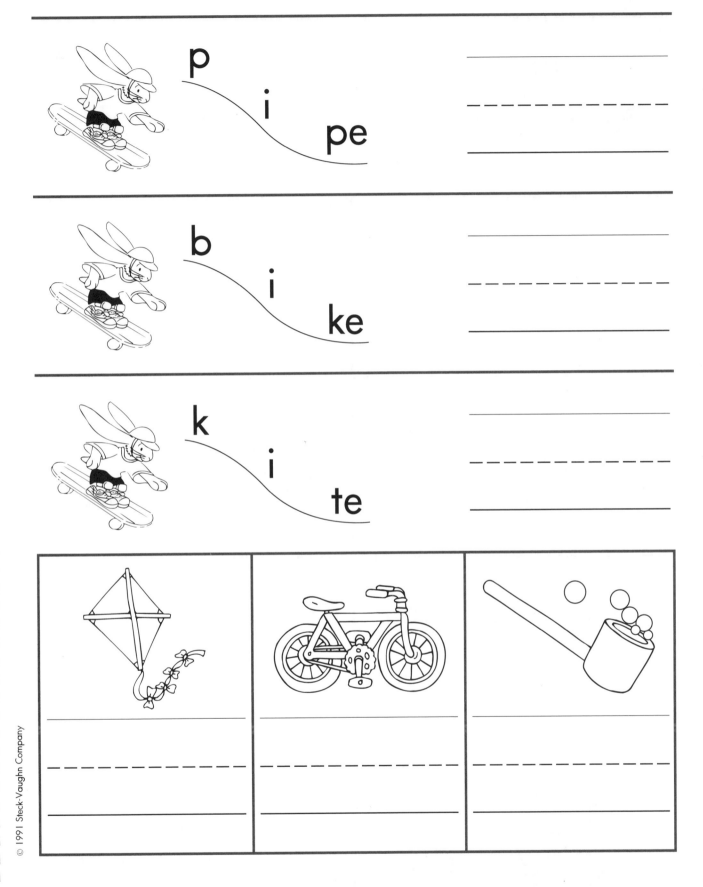

p i pe

_____
- - - - - - - - -
_____

b i ke

_____
- - - - - - - - -
_____

k i te

_____
- - - - - - - - -
_____

_____
- - - - - - - - -
_____

_____
- - - - - - - - -
_____

_____
- - - - - - - - -
_____

Name _____

Blending Long i Words Blend each word, and write it on the line. Then write the word that names each picture.

m i ce _____

5 five
fin

9 nine
nip

kite
kid

bit
bike

dig
dive

pipe
pin

dime
dig

win
vine

Recognizing Long i Words Blend and write the first word. Then circle the word that names each picture.

Mike has a fine _____.

kite   kit

The kite is up in a _____.

pin   pine

Mike got it with a _____.

line   lid

He put the kite on a _____.

bib   bike

Name _____

Completing Long i Sentences   Write the word on the line that completes each sentence.

Mike has a nice bike.
Dave has nine dimes.

Jake hikes for a mile.
Kate will hide the kite.

Pam will like to ride.
Five mice bite the ham.

A vine is on the pine.
Mike dives for a dime.

Long i Sentences   Underline the sentence that tells about each picture.

O 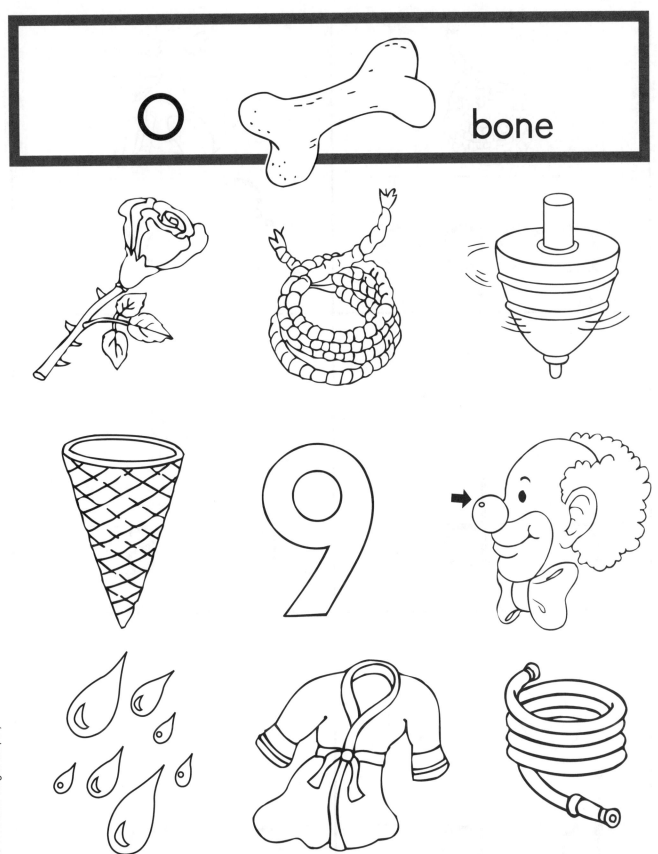 bone

Name _____

Long o (cvce) Color the pictures whose names have the long *o* sound.

23

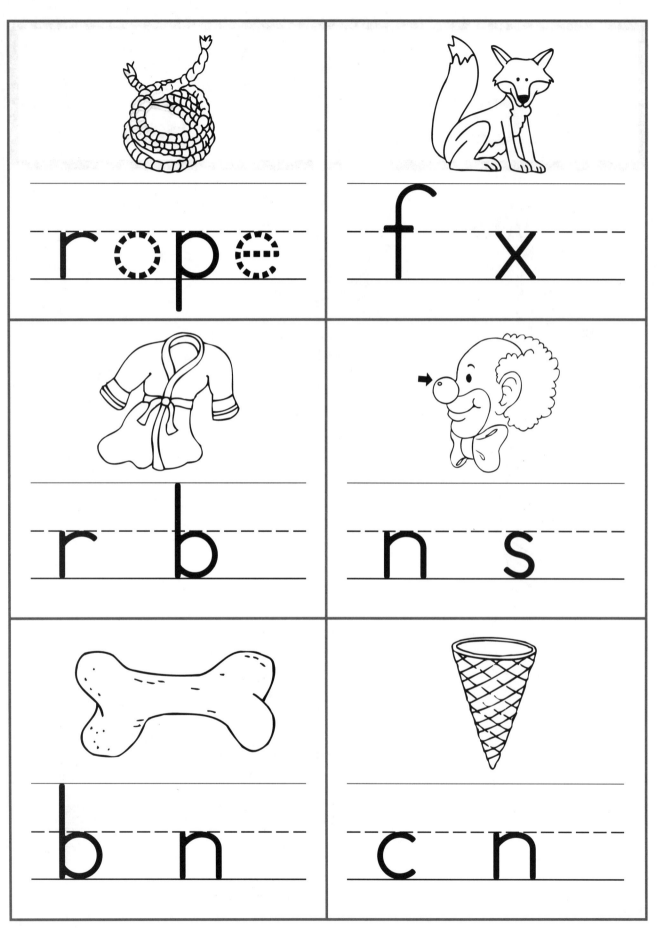

r o p e

f _ _ x

r _ _ b

n _ _ s

b _ _ n

c _ _ n

Completing Long o Words (cvce) Write *o_e* to complete each word whose name has the long *o* sound.

O   goat

Long o (oa) Color the pictures whose names have the long o sound.

s o a p

t ___ d

t ___ p

c ___ t

b ___ t

g ___ t

26   **Completing Long o Words (oa)**   Write *oa* to complete each word whose name has the long *o* sound.

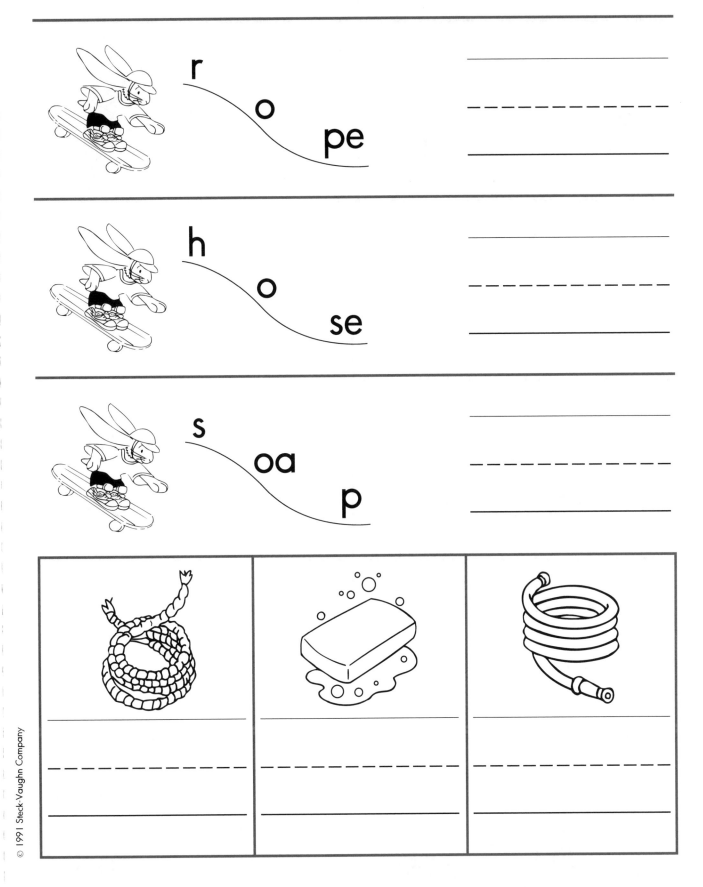

r   o   pe

h   o   se

s   oa   p

Name _____

Blending Long o Words   Blend each word, and write it on the line. Then write the word that names each picture.

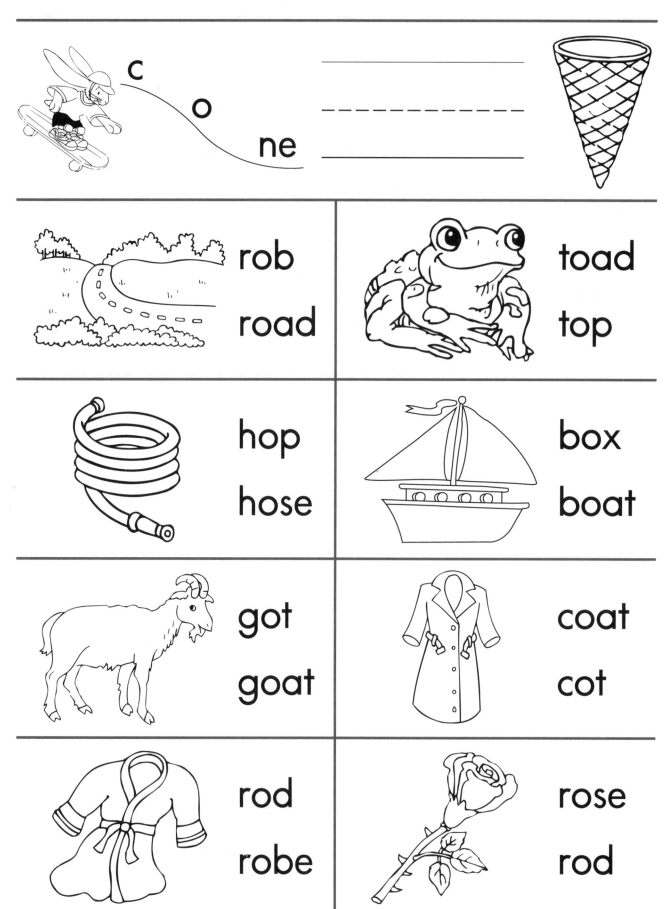

c

o

ne

rob	toad
road	top
hop	box
hose	boat
got	coat
goat	cot
rod	rose
robe	rod

Recognizing Long o Words Blend and write the first word. Then circle the word that names each picture.

A dog has a big _____.

box   bone

It digs in the _____.

hole   hog

A _____ pokes up its nose.

top   toad

The hole is its _____.

hop   home

Name _____

Completing Long o Sentences Write the word on the line that completes each sentence.

The hose is on the road.
Tug the boat with rope.

The goat is on a rope.
The toad is on a rose.

His nose is in a rose.
The hose is at home.

Ron rode to his home.
Tom loans Joan a coat.

Long o Sentences Underline the sentence that tells about each picture.

u   cube

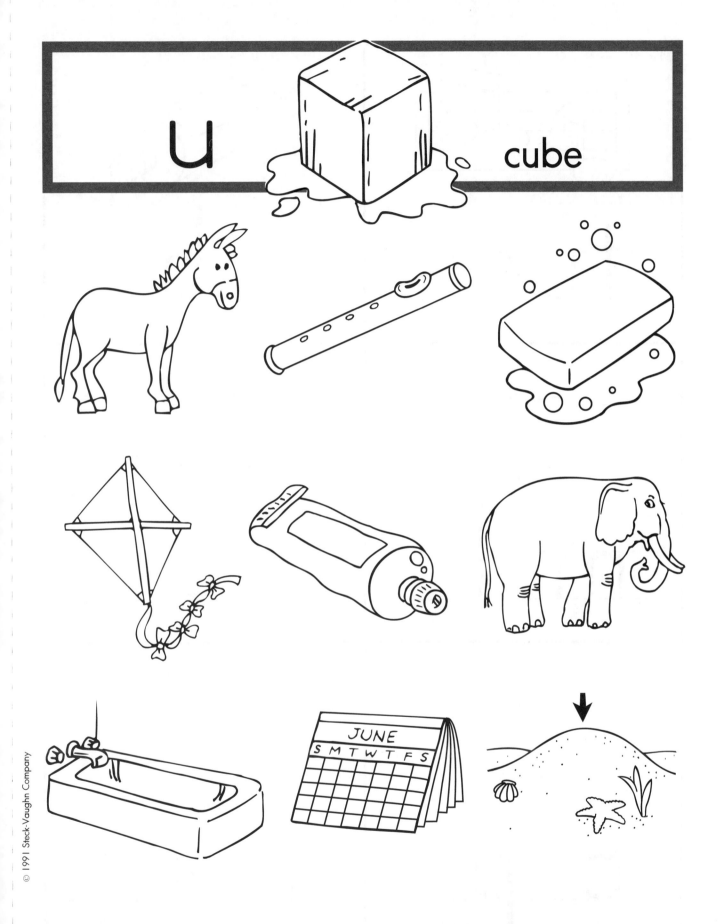

Long u (cvce)   Color the pictures whose names have the long *u* sound.

t u n e

t ___ b

m ___ l

c ___ b

c ___ p

f ___ s

Completing Long u Words (cvce) Write *u_e* to complete each word whose name has the long *u* sound.

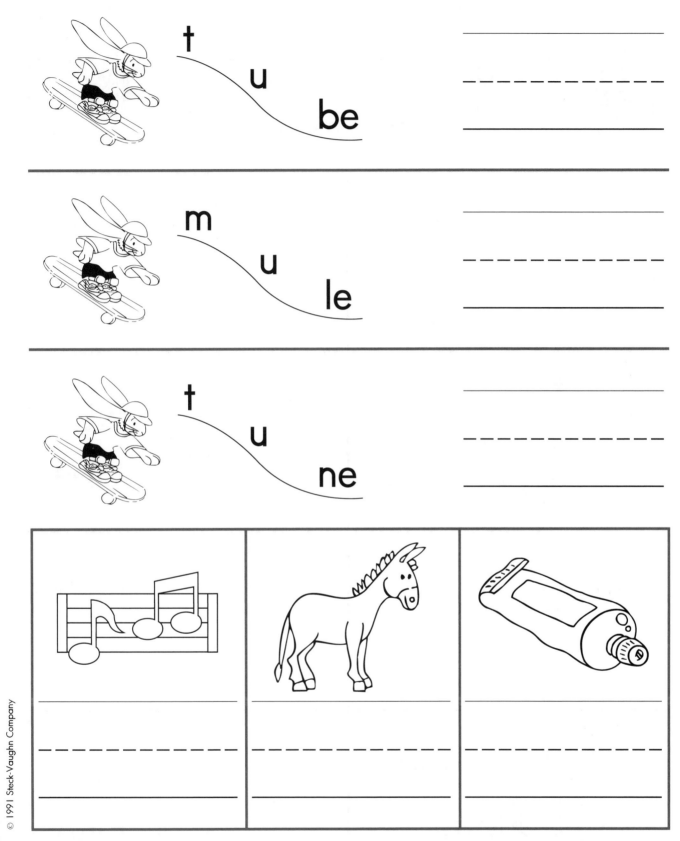

t u be

m u le

t u ne

Name _____

Blending Long u Words   Blend each word, and write it on the line. Then write the word that names each picture.

33

t

u

ne

_____

- -

_____

mud mule	fun fuse
dune dug	tug tube
jug June	huge hum
cube cut	tub tune

Recognizing Long u Words Blend and write the first word. Then circle the word that names each picture.

June has a _____ pal.

cut   cute

Luke has a big _____.

mule   mud

They go to a _____ fair.

hug   huge

The mule gets a _____.

cube   cub

Name _____

Completing Long u Sentences Write the word on the line that completes each sentence.

The dune is huge.
The mule is on a box.

Luke rides in a tube.
June will hum a tune.

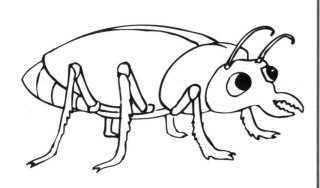

A huge bug is not cute.
Luke is on the dune.

Duke has a cute cub.
June got a cube.

e

bee

Name _____

Long e (ee)   Color the pictures whose names have the long e sound.

37

h ee l

p _ _ n

p _ _ l

f _ _ t

s _ _ d

j _ _ p

38   **Completing Long e Words (ee)**   *Write* ee *to complete each word whose name has the long e sound.*

e  leaf

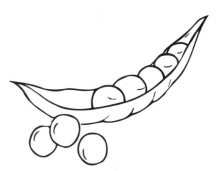

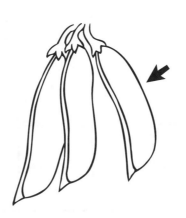

Name _____

Long e (ea)   Color the pictures whose names have the long e sound.

b e a k

l __ __ f

10

t __ __ n

m __ __ t

p __ __ s

s __ __ l

40   **Completing Long e Words (ea)**   Write *ea* to complete each word whose name has the long *e* sound.

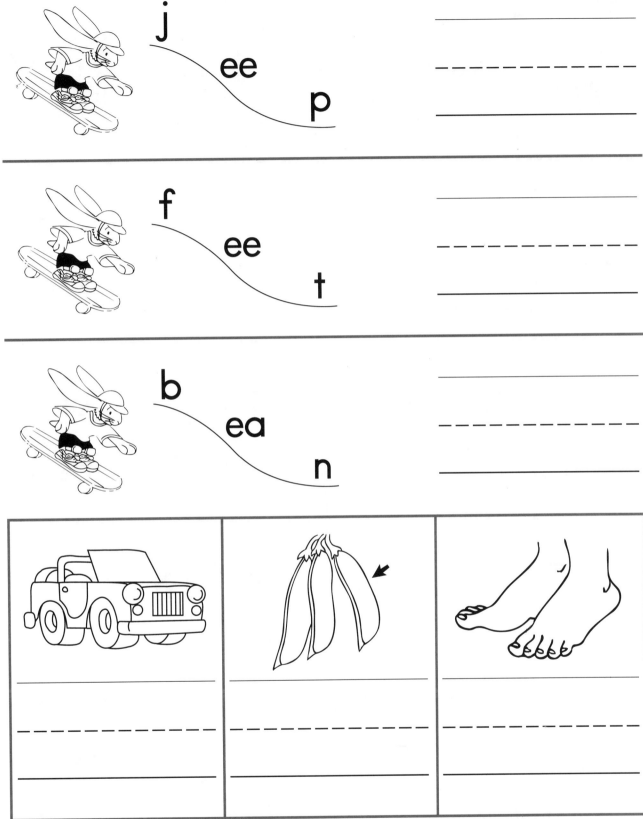

j ee p

f ee t

b ea n

Name _____

Blending Long e Words   Blend each word, and write it on the line. Then write the word that names each picture.

p

ea

s

_____

- - - - - - - - - -

_____

fed
feet

leaf
leg

seal
set

jet
jeep

men
meat

beak
bed

pet
peel

hen
heel

Recognizing Long e Words *Blend and write the first word. Then circle the word that names each picture.*

The team will eat a _____.

meal   men

Lee will take _____.

men   meat

Bea will like the _____.

beet   bed

The team will _____ fine.

fun   feel

Name _____

Completing Long e Sentences   Write the word on the line that completes each sentence.

A bee is on the leaf.

A seal is in the sea.

Bea did not eat a seed.

Beans are a fine meal.

The team will read.

The team eats meat.

Lee got the peel.

The heat pipe leaks.

Long e Sentences Underline the sentence that tells about each picture.

peas pipe pail	cake cone cube
soap seed safe	sail seal soap
mail mule meat	like leaf lake
beak bake bike	robe rain read
toad tune tail	hair heel hose

Name _____

Reviewing Long Vowel Words   Circle the word that names each picture.

A _____ needs to eat.

mule   mug

Five mice see a _____.

fan   face

A wet nose hits the _____.

mice   mitt

A rose makes a safe _____.

hop   home

Reviewing Long Vowel Sentences Write the word on the line that completes each sentence.

Kate rides in the rain.
June hikes to the lake.

The mule has a load.
Jean paid for the tube.

Gail got a rain cape.
Joan tapes the hose.

A seed is in his beak.
Five mice eat the seeds.

Name _____

Reviewing Long Vowel Sentences Underline the sentence that tells about each picture.

A Huge Meal

Kate has a cute goat.

The goat likes to eat.

He ate a hose, a tube, and nine pipes.

Kate gave him beans and beets.

Will he wait to eat?

Reviewing Long Vowels in a Story Read the story, and underline each word that has a long vowel sound.